INVESTING SECRETS

FOR A

CHAMPAGNE LIFE

CASSIE PARKS

Cover and Interior Design: John H. Matthews
Editing: Cynthia Kane

Author's photo courtesy of Aimee Starr

ADVANCE PRAISE

To be honest, I've been reading invest-in-real-estate books for years, ever since Rich Dad, Poor Dad came out. But I've never... you know, actually invested.

Often (being even more honest here), I wouldn't even finish the book. I'd find them either too light in the useful-information department, or so heavy with figures and formulas that it would make the entire prospect of buying a rental property utterly overwhelming.

"Investing Secrets For A Champagne Life" is nothing like that.

Cassie has written a how-to guide that is encouraging , realistic and ruthlessly practical. She gives you a candid report of her journey from novice to pro investor, with clear and insightful guidance on the lessons learned in between.

If you want the numbers, she's got them. If you want all the options, she's got those too.

And if you're looking for inspiration from a woman who retired at 32, she's got that too.

Believe me, this is much more than a real-estate-investment manual, it's a life-style manifesto.

It will be your go-to reference as you build your Champagne Life portfolio. I can say that with confidence because it's rapidly become mine.

Jacquelinie Gates
Goddess. Coach. Nest Awesomizer
www.jacqueline-gates.com

This book on real estate investing is very inspiring and gave me some ideas for saving for my down payment. I never would have thought of the creative ways I can use resources I already have and how I can apply them to my real estate investing goals.

Skye Frank

I met Cassie at an open house just weeks after she retired at 32. I was amazed! I am her realtor (Brandon from the book). I have spent countless hours with Cassie watching her grow her real estate empire. Even though I am a realtor, I have learned a lot from her in the time we've known each other. She inspires me. I often ask, "How can I be you (Cassie) quicker?"

When you read a book, sometimes you wonder if the person really did it like they said they did. I can attest Cassie knows her stuff and she follows her own advice when it comes to real estate. If you want to get started investing in real estate, create a plan to retire early, or just make a lot of money, start by reading Investing Secrets for a Champagne Life.

Brandon Beston

brandonbeston.kwrealty.com

This book presents a great case for real estate investing and has me excited! It covers everything you need to get started including, most importantly, the mindset to do it right. This is a book I will re-read before investing. It is invaluable particularly for people new to real estate and is packed with practical and useful information - this is quite possibly the only book potential investors might need to read on the subject.

Stacey Gower

Where was Cassie Parks the first time around when I was buying my first property?!

Cassie takes the time to guide the reader through the ins and outs of real estate investment with tips both the practical and inspirational in mind.

A definite keeper of a book and I am keeping it on hand when I purchase my next property.

Nikki Davis

Before reading Investing Secrets for a Champagne Life I knew nothing about how to get started in real estate investing... and by nothing I mean I didn't know which questions to ask to even start learning. It was a very intimidated subject for me. It just felt like a secret language with lots of columns of numbers that I didn't know how to translate. I am so happy to have discovered Cassie's book because she lays out the beginning steps, the process, the ways to buy, provides a glossary and resources, and even crunches the numbers in a friendly, non-intimidating way. I still have a lot more to learn but I feel more confident that I know how to begin investing in real estate. If you have always been interested in real estate but just didn't know where to begin, this book is an invaluable tool to get to you started in the right direction. I feel like Dorothy taking her first steps down the yellow brick road!

Sara Cuthbert

To my mom, for not only introducing me to real estate, but more importantly, for teaching and modeling that every woman has the power to take responsibility for her financial success.

TABLE OF CONTENTS

CHAPTER 1
A CASE FOR INVESTING IN REAL ESTATE

This morning, I woke up, and I got to choose what I wanted to do with my day. I run a business, so there are a few things I want to get done for the day, but it's always what I want to do. I run my business the way I want to. I do the things I love doing and I travel when I want. Two-hour lunches are a must. All of this was made possible because I took the leap and took my financial future into my own hands. I became a real estate investor.

What is a real estate investor? The simple definition is someone who invests in real estate, but it's more than that. A real estate investor is a badass. Why? Because they aren't willing to settle for the traditional way. They want more. They don't want to just sock their money away in a 401(k), and hope all the retirement calculators are right.

You know what I'm talking about, if you want to retire making x then you need to save y a month from now until you're 67. Don't forget to cross your fingers and hope it all works out. Hope you picked the right stocks. Hope your mutual fund doesn't go belly up. I remember in the early 2000s, when there were a couple of mutual funds that went out of business and some people lost everything. Those people technically did it right. In fact, the family I'm thinking of probably was frugal, and I'm sure they saved more than enough, and overnight it was gone. That thought always remains in the back of my mind.

It's that thought, among others, that led me to find a different path. I'm lucky enough to have had a mom who pointed me toward that path. If you didn't, follow me. I want to introduce you to a secret that not very many people know about, or are not brave enough to follow through on.

The secret? Investing in real estate to create wealth and financial freedom. How do I know it works? Because I've leveraged the power of real estate investing to create my financial freedom to ensure I never have to go back to work again. Now, you may love your job and that's great! No matter how much you love it, I'm guessing you don't want to work forever.

I'm also guessing you're a smart, savvy, woman (I apologize to the men reading his book. I am so happy you are.) You're probably investing in your 401(k) at work. You might even have an IRA, too. Congratulations and great job! The first step to creating wealth and financial independence is starting. Taking advantage of your 401(k) and possibly an IRA is a great start to ensure you can retire someday.

If for some reason you're not investing in your 401(k) right now, stop reading this and go figure out how to get started. If your company matches a portion of your contributions (let's say 3%) then you want to be contributing a minimum of 3% to your 401(k). Why? Because if you don't, you're missing out on free money. It's always a good idea to invest the amount your company will match. If you're concerned you might lose money, talk to your 401(k) advisor or put it in the most conservative choice. You may even want to put it in a money market. No matter what, take advantage of the free money.

Back to our regularly scheduled programming. So you have a 401(k) you're investing in at work, possibly 401(k) you rolled over from other jobs, and you might even have an IRA you started on your own. How do you feel about them? Are you tracking them? Do you make changes or understand how your money is growing, if it is? Do you even open the statements? Do you know if you're doing enough to reach your retirement goals?

Or did you do what most people do, fill out the form to enroll and then guess what investments you should pick? Most people just make picks because they have to and then don't ever go back and look at them. Why? Because you're not a stockbroker. You have a job that is a reflection of your skill set and not the stock market. You have a lot going on. You know maybe you should call and ask for help picking stocks and mutual funds, but either you don't have time or you're not sure you'd understand what they're saying anyway. For whatever reason, you just don't do it.

At one point in my life, I worked for a financial services company, so I have a better understanding of mutual funds than most – and even I didn't really know what I was doing when I picked my funds. I had reasons why I picked them, but I'm not sure they were really good reasons. It's how the system is set up. Sure, there's help available, but few people take advantage of it for one reason or another. I'm not saying that's a good thing. Whether you decide to invest in real estate at the end of this book or not, my intention is that you commit to taking a more active role in your financial future.

When I worked for a financial services company, I was taught you want a 12% rate of return because then your money doubles every six years. I've done the math, and looked at my investments that are in the stock market. They haven't averaged 12%. Now, mutual fund experts would say I need to wait longer and average the return. I don't know about you, but I've never been good at waiting and hoping.

Here's an interesting fact, considering I was taught at a financial services company that you want to be getting a 12% return on your investment (ROI). Historically the S&P 500 has an average rate of return of 11% before taxes and 8% after tax. Eight to eleven percent isn't terrible. It's going to beat inflation, but I want better. I've never been one to settle for average.

The thing I dislike about the market, other than the less than desirable returns, is that I have to trust someone else. I have a good memory and I still remember that couple that lost everything. I prefer to have more control over my money and how much it's making.

What's the secret to having more control and making a better ROI? Real estate. A seasoned investor can make more than 20% a year on their money. I think if you are smart, do your homework, and work with the right people, anyone can make a 10% rate of return, after taxes. When I started, I had no idea what I was doing, or why I was doing it. I started about six years ago. I am currently making a 36% ROI on the money I've invested in real estate.

When I say I had no idea what I was doing, I really mean I had no idea what I was doing. If I had to do it over again, I would do some things differently. The one thing I would never change is getting started. Every breakdown, heartache, stressful moment of my real estate career has only made me smarter, more confident, more determined and most importantly more wealthy.

Financial independence, making enough passive income to cover my monthly expenses, so I can choose whether or not I want to go to work, was a non-negotiable for me. It was my goal, my intention, my dream, my do or die trying. There's power in being able to take care of yourself financially. Money isn't everything, but it provides a freedom. Freedom is one of my core values, which means it's very important to me.

Hint: Knowing your core values will help you determine your *why* for investing in real estate, which I'll talk about further along in the book. If you don't know your core values, check out the resources section.

Because becoming financially independent was my dream, I started young. I learned about compound interest when I was 19, and because of that, I started investing in my first IRA. I wanted to be financially independent so badly that it was worth it to save every month, and I was prepared to wait until I was 62. I did what my financial plan said, and I started saving and investing in my IRA.

I saved up my first hundred dollars when I was 10, and my mom took me to the bank so I could open a savings account. When I was 19, I went to work for a financial services company. Sales isn't my thing, but I loved learning all about finances. I started my first IRA while I worked for the financial services company. I had learned that if you start investing early, you have to invest less, because there's more time for your money to grow. When I started at a job with a 401(k), of course I signed up. And I invested 10% of my monthly salary into my 401(k).

I had a goal, and more importantly, a dream to retire and live a good life, so of course I did all the things I was "supposed" to do in order to get there. But I've never been one to just do it like you're supposed to. That is how I got into real estate investing. I wanted to make more money, faster, and I wanted to have more of it at retirement and I saw real estate as the way to make that happen.

Eventually, once I got into real estate investing and started learning more and experiencing success, my new goal and dream became to retire as quickly as possible. It didn't take long before intention, determination, and utilizing my deliberate creation skills, led to everything magically falling into place quickly, and my being able to retire at 32. (If you're interested in the role the Law of Attraction played in my success, check out the free audio available here liveyourchampagnelife.com/investing-gifts)

There's the rush of excitement I get when I buy a new investment, especially now that I buy really cool places. Once you get the hang of this stuff, you know what forms are coming and what signing your name means. The excitement builds until the final page, and then you look at your realtor, and he hands you a present. You open the beautifully wrapped gift bag and find a gift certificate for a 2-hour massage at one of the most luxurious spas in Denver. You skip, like an excited child, out of the closing – because it's the 30th, and tomorrow, on the 1st, you'll get a check for rent on your new investment. It starts making money less than 24 hours after you purchased it. That's my kind of investment.

A little over a month later, you find yourself back at the title company with coffee and a chocolate chip cookie signing on yet another property. This one is extra special. This one is special because it doesn't require a loan. You're paying for it with the profit from the sale of two of your other properties. In a matter of a month, you've managed to lower your debt to income ratio and double what you were previously making.

This property needs work, so you head over to get started. There's something magical about putting in some of the work on your investments yourself. It's not for everyone, but sometimes it just feels good to put your sweat into the process of turning something that was *okay* into something that is beautiful and is going to make you lots of money.

The more successful I get in real estate, the less "work" I do, but every once in awhile it feels good. Especially on this property, because it reminds me how far I've come. I could have hired someone to paint, but in many ways I consider it an act of love. It's part of my process for setting the intention for who's going to live there, and the experience I desire to have with the property.

It's best not to get attached to a property, but it's a must to appreciate it. It represents my dream and my freedom. This investment is one of the reasons I get to spend my days building my business, knowing there's always money coming in. There's nothing better than when your phone starts dinging on the first because everyone is paying rent. Is there anything sweeter than money coming in? For me, there is. The freedom to go to brunch with your mom on a Tuesday or go to your Goddaughter's field trip, or go visit your niece on her birthday, all without asking a boss for time off. The freedom and possibility that comes with the money is priceless.

There's a freedom in knowing someone else is making a payment for you. In fifteen to thirty years there will be more money. More money to live a more fun life traveling around. Possibly to help those you love go to college or get their own investment property. Maybe to fund their dream trip to Europe or to help out someone you love. That feeling is pretty amazing too.

The value of your investment might go down on paper, and you might make less in rent one year, but it's still going to make money while the value climbs back up. If you're invested in a mutual fund or with a stockbroker, you're still going to have to pay them a fee when your investment value declines, and there's no guarantee it will come back. You just have to wait and see. There's no guarantee the value of a property will come back either, but it will never disappear on you.

When you invest in real estate, you make a real time estimate of what your rate of return is going to be. If you do your homework and make good choices, you set yourself up for success rather than looking at historical averages and hoping they hold true. Historically, the S&P has made 11% before taxes and 8% after taxes. Seasoned real estate investors can make 25%. Right now my ROI, return on investment, for the money I've invested in real estate is 36% and I didn't really know what I was doing until recently.

One of the coolest things about real estate is that rent keeps up with inflation. In 30 years, rent is going to be similar to what it is in today's dollars. Meaning you don't have to plan for your investment to keep up with inflation. That's built in. If I'm making $4000 today in rent, I'll be making the equivalent in 30 years.

Real estate also has the added bonus of appreciation. In Denver, the average rate of appreciation for real estate is 6% since 1971. Appreciation is a bonus because you make investments that are good without counting on appreciation. That means you're not sitting around crossing your fingers and hoping that your property will go up in value.

What your investment is worth doesn't matter as much as what it makes each month. Wouldn't it be nice to still make money while your investment is down? From 2010-2013, when I opened my property tax bills, I wouldn't even look at the value of my property because it was so much lower than what I paid for it. I also knew it didn't matter, because I was making the most I'd ever made from the property. Wouldn't it be nice to still make money even if your investment drops in value?

All of these are the magical secrets of real estate that someone has probably never shared with you. I believe they are the secrets that need to be shared with smart, savvy woman who want to take responsibility for their financial futures. I believe that should be every woman. I start sharing these secrets early. In fact, on my Goddaughter's 6th birthday celebration, I started teaching her about investing in real estate. By happenstance I had a property to go see, which I purchased, on her birthday. I'm not sure she remembers, but I don't think it's ever too early to start teaching a girl or a woman how to take control of her financial future. The good news is it's never too late either. You can start investing in real estate right where you are at whatever age you are right now.

Now that you know the secret to greater wealth and financial freedom, are you ready to learn more? Like, how to get started, and how to evaluate a property? If you'd like to know how to get started, even if it doesn't seem possible, follow me through the next pages. I'll teach you some of my biggest lessons and the biggest secrets I've learned.

CHAPTER 2
GETTING READY TO INVEST

As I said, when I started, I really didn't know what I was doing. In the beginning, it just sort of happened – and as time passed, I became more conscious in my choices and decisions. I defined my goals and desired outcomes. The more I did, the more I learned – and the better I got.

In the pages following this one, information is going to be coming at you really fast. And by really fast, I mean like Dale Earnhardt Jr. is coming around the corner. It might feel a little scary – like taking a corner at 180 MPH. The most important thing is to finish the book. By finishing the book, you're going to have a really good foundation. Then you can come back and go through the book step-by-step. If you don't know anything about investing in real estate, that's okay. In the next chapters, I am going to walk you through the basics and point you in the right direction for any next steps you desire to take.

Investing in real estate isn't a get rich quick plan. It's a long-term investment of time, energy and money. It's important, as you go through the book, to remember that. You don't have to figure out how to build your empire in the next hour; you just have to make a decision as to whether you want to build one.

Real estate investing isn't for everyone. There's a reason the returns are higher. There is more of an investment in learning and understanding. If you have enough cash, you can invest it right away, but if you don't have enough cash to purchase a property, there are loans to be secured and understood. You might also need to save up, or investigate other funding sources.

Take your time in the entire process. Make sure you understand what's being presented. I am going to present some non-traditional methods and ways of looking at things. I always point you to the people you want to go to for more guidance. Use them. Ask questions. Get the clarity you need to make good choices and decisions that support your goals and dreams.

If you do it on your own and figure everything out for yourself, you'll probably be successful. If you enroll help and create a team, you're much more likely to be successful. I'm telling you everything I know because I want you to be able to be more successful, faster than I was. I also want you to experience less frustration, fear and doubt.

If I was to do it over, following my own advice, I could do it with less stress and probably be more successful, quicker. Retired at 32 is pretty good, but my wish for you is that my journey can make yours easier. I want to share everything I have learned with you so that when you come up against something, you can say to yourself, "She talked about this in the book," and then you can pull the book out and find the shortcuts for what to do next.

If at the end of this book you decide you want to invest in real estate, that's awesome. Really be clear and feel good about this decision.

If there is any part of you that doesn't want to do it, that's okay. Honor that. The people that get chewed up and spit out in the real estate investing business are the ones that only go in half way. They want to do it, but they're scared – and they never let go of that fear. That fear keeps them in a loop – being scared that attracts more reasons to be scared. It leads to frustration and making bad decisions. If at the end of this book there isn't something inside screaming, "Hell yes, I have to figure it out" then investing in real estate probably isn't for you and that's okay. Honor that.

Now, if at the end of this book, your eyes are crossed, your brain is spinning and you're thinking, "I have to do this," that's awesome. The next step will be to take some sort of action, like setting up a savings account or opening up your investment statements. Taking that small action will get you moving in the direction you want to go.

If the answer is "hell yes," and you're scared, that's okay. Do you remember being a kid and waiting in line for the roller coaster? You knew you wanted to do it. You knew you had to do it. But it scared the shit out of you? That's likely how you're going to feel when you get to the end of the book, which is so exciting.

Knowing you want to do something, and acknowledging that it's scary, is a great way to manage fear. Whenever it seems scary, you can return to the fact in your gut you knew it was right. That lets you know you're on the right path. Fear is often your brain just needing more knowledge. If you feel fear, ease it by getting more knowledge. Try rereading the book, calling a realtor, or a Certified Public Accountant (CPA) to explore your ideas. Try analyzing the numbers around your ideas. Perhaps ensuring you have a cushion of money will make you feel safe and empowered. The safer and more empowered you feel, the more success you will experience. That goes for anything and everything.

Make it a habit to make financial decisions and take actions regarding your finances from inspiration rather than desperation. Acting from inspiration happens when you think about who you want to be and what you want to experience. It comes from putting yourself in that place of having, being and doing – whatever that is. When you put yourself in the place of having, being and doing what you desire, and you follow the intuitive nudges – or inspired actions, as I like to call them – that follow, you're acting from inspiration.

Acting From Inspiration	Inspired Real Estate Examples	Acting From Desperation	Desperate Real Estate Examples
Follow intuitive nudges	Walk into an open house, leisurely start looking for places in an area	Rationalizing	Running the numbers in a way that you get the outcome you want instead of what's actually true
Feeling calm, peaceful, certain	Thoroughly investigating a property from a logical place	Feeling intense, nervous, uncertain	Not being able to sleep, feeling anxious
Taking inspired action	Calling a loan officer or realtor when it feels good	Jumping in without thinking	Not properly investigating a property and its risks and potential
Confidence	Total certainty in your decision	Anxiety	Continually questioning your decision
Honoring your intuition	Saying no to opportunities that your intuition says aren't good	Ignoring your gut instinct or intuition	Purchasing a property when your intuition says not to
Staying true to your desired goals.	Saying yes, when a property is in alignment with your goals and no when it's not	Ignoring your goals or going for the get rich quick option	Making a purchase or an offer, when the numbers aren't in alignment with your goals
Feeling abundant	Knowing if one place doesn't work out, they'll be another one	Feeling desperate	Thinking "this place" has to work out because there will never be another one this good

When you think about what you want, and then decide you have to have it *right now* and you just start doing things you *think* will work to get it, that's acting from desperation. Anytime you have to rationalize a decision or action, it was probably born out of desperation. If you are in such a hurry that you can't stop and do what you know you probably should do, or you've been advised to do, you're probably acting in desperation. If you're ignoring your gut feelings, you're definitely following desperation.

Whether you invest in real estate or not, the greatest thing you can ever do to ensure your financial success is to learn the difference between inspiration and desperation and then to train yourself to only follow your inspiration. If you only take away one thing from this book, my greatest desire would be that it's a commitment to *only* follow your inspiration.

Learning to hear and feel the difference between inspiration and desperation can take practice. If you're ever not sure, walk away. Be willing to let go. What you're actually letting go of is the murkiness. When you let go, you're inviting clarity in. If you let go and you feel relief or ambivalence, your gut was telling you no. If you walk away and there's a nagging little voice telling you to go back or ask a question or look at it again, that's your intuition leading you back. It's your intuition needing an answer before it can make the decision. If you walk away and you get that nagging feeling that you have to do it, listen. Inspiration is often soft. It doesn't yell. It might quietly nag, but it doesn't yell. It doesn't feel like pressure. It feels like excitement. As you learn to trust your inspiration and identify desperation, it gets easier to navigate.

I've made only one real estate decision from the desperation place – and it didn't work out all that great. In the end, I was lucky and it worked out okay, but it took years for it to *really* work out. It caused a lot of extra stress, anger and frustration in my life. I learned from that one time that I didn't want to repeat that mistake.

Now if something feels off, or if anything isn't a *hell yes*, I walk away. Sometimes walking away I realize I feel relieved and I know it wasn't going to be a good investment for me. Sometimes walking away allows for questions to surface or things that need to be investigated. Once I've gotten the answer, sometimes "I don't know" turns into a "yes," and sometimes it turns into a solid "no." Be willing to walk away and trust that if whatever it is doesn't work out, something better is right behind it. Being willing to walk away makes you more powerful both personally and in negotiations.

There's always another possibility. Looking back, it's easy to see how – if I would have said yes to certain things that didn't feel good – I would have missed some really great opportunities. Make a commitment to yourself *right now* to honor your intuition and your gut instinct. Make a promise to yourself to follow your inspiration, and let everything else go. Now buckle up – because it's time to talk real estate investing.

Before You Get Started Make Sure To:
- Define your goals
- Make a commitment to the long term for investing
- Give yourself permission to take time and learn
- Make a decision that feels good
- Commit to honoring your intuition and following your inspiration

CHAPTER 3
GETTING STARTED

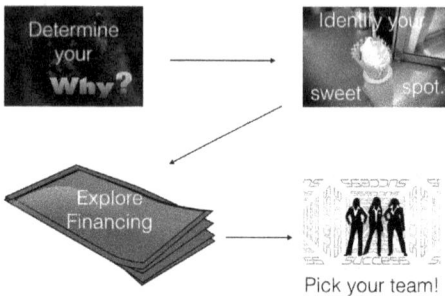

Determine your **Why?** → Identify your sweet spot.

Explore Financing → Pick your team!

Determine Your Why

The first thing you need to do as a real estate investor is decide WHY you are investing. When I got started I did it for the same reason most people do, I thought it was a way to make money. Although she never really talked about her rental properties, my mom had them when I was growing up. (My parents are married, but my dad will tell you that those are her houses.) In my early twenties, I realized how much the houses were worth compared to what she paid for them. Then I thought about how much time she had invested in them over the years. It wasn't really that much time, when you looked at it in comparison to the amount they added to her net worth. That's when I realized I wanted a rental house.

My mom had gone into real estate by accident. My parents found a bigger, better house they could afford, but it was in 1990, and the real estate market had fallen. The house we moved out of wasn't worth what my parents had paid for it. Instead of taking the hit, they decided to rent it out. I also "accidentally" got started in real estate too. My sister and I attempted to flip a house. Everything didn't go as planned, and we had a house that we couldn't sell for what we needed to, so my mom and I bought it together as an investment property.

If I had it to do over again, I wouldn't have invested in the flip property to begin with. I would have taken the money I invested in the flip, and purchased an investment property straight out. You live and learn. This first house got me started, and helped me learn the ropes of being a real estate investor. It also fulfilled my dream of having some passive income. It was only $100 a month, but that was the easiest $100 I was making at the time.

In the beginning of my investing career, I didn't really know what I was doing. Actually, to be clear, I had *absolutely no idea* what I was doing. I knew it sounded pretty good to have a house that someone else was paying the mortgage on for me, while I was pocketing a little change. In 30 years, after the mortgage was paid off, I'd be making more money. At that time that sounded pretty good.

Fast forward to now, and I may or may not have invested in that property. I had about $18,000 invested into that property, and I was making about $100 a month. That's about 6.7% on my money. Not bad, but not great either. I'm telling you this because so many people jump into real estate because they think it's how you build wealth or because they need to diversify. Like me, they don't really know *why* they are doing it. To build wealth is a good reason, but it's a little ambiguous.

Let's assume the overall reason you're investing in real estate is because you feel like it's better than investing more of your money in the market. The main reason is because you desire to make more money from your money. But I want you to further determine your *why*, because it's what is going to guide your decisions and set you up for success.

The first reason people invest in real estate is for appreciation. Their intention is to buy a property, hold it for a certain amount of time, and sell it for a higher price. I would say this is the most risky – and seems a lot like investing in the market to me. You have to time things really well, and you run the risk of being wrong and losing a lot of money. Hindsight is 20/20 and everyone thinks looking back they could have predicted a crash. However, when you're in the middle of it, it can be harder to see. I prefer to have more control and feel more confident about my investment choices.

The second reason to invest in real estate is for the long term. This is where you're investing in a property as your retirement fund. You'll likely want to make enough each month to cover expenses and repairs, but you don't care if you're making extra money each month because your goal is to be making money 30 years from now, when you are ready to retire. You're happy to just have someone else make the payment for you while you continue to work and support yourself.

This is a great retirement strategy. Depending on your income, a handful of these and thirty years from now, you'll be set. In this case, you're just looking to make sure you can rent the place to cover the payment, any repairs that need to be done, and a management company if you desire. The money you invest for down payments will pay off in the long term when you're retired and living off the rent.

The third reason people invest in real estate is to get a better, more consistent rate of return on their money. Real estate is uniquely different from the stock market because in many cases, you can invest some of your money and take advantage of a loan from a bank, which can help you increase your rate of return. By rate of return I mean the percentage of the money that you invested that you are earning each year.

Example:

If you invested $25,000 and made $2,500 a year, you would be making a 10% return on your investment. You get that number by dividing $2,500 by $25,000, which equals 10%.

In this example, if you have a loan, you're actually making more than 10% because someone else is paying your mortgage, which is paying down the principal balance. I like to think of that as bonus money. The other bonus is appreciation. If the property goes up in value, you're adding to your net worth.

Real estate is unique because you can take a loan for your investment. For $25,000, you can likely invest in a $100,000 property. This is fabulous, because you get to take advantage of any appreciation and the fact that the principal loan balance is being lowered every month. In this case, you have the potential to make money three ways. If you're investing for a better rate of return, you save the money you make each month and then reinvest it in another property, or add any additional money (above all the expenses) to the principal so you're paying the house off faster.

The fourth reason people invest in real estate is for cash flow. By *cash flow*, I mean the amount of money you're making (net) each month. Honestly, I think this is the most exciting reason. Cash flow and better return on your investment are very similar reasons. The difference is your intended goal. Personally, I invested for the better rate of return and kept reinvesting because I wanted to create a passive income I could live off of, which would give me the freedom to quit my job.

When you invest for cash flow, you're looking at how much you will net (how much is remaining after all the expenses are paid) from a property on a monthly or yearly basis. You're still looking at how much you can make on the amount of money you invest, but your plan is to use it on a monthly basis to live on, rather than invest in an additional property. You may start out being an investor for the better rate of return, and then evolve to reason number four over time as you invest more and more. This is a great retirement strategy, and you get the advantage of appreciation and someone else making a payment for you as well if you take out a loan.

Why are you going to invest in real estate? Take a few minutes to think about it and make a decision as to what best suites your desires.

What Is Your Why?			
Appreciation	Long Term Investing	Better Rate of Return	Cash Flow

Financing

Now that you know WHY you are going to start investing in real estate, let's talk about what you're going to need to get started. If any of these terms are unfamiliar, refer to the glossary in the back. First, if you're going to invest using a mortgage, you're going to need to get a loan. To get the loan is going to require fairly good credit, and a debt to income ratio that is low enough to add additional debt. Now that you are a real estate investor, you want to leave as much room open for someone to give you a loan as possible. What I mean by that is keep your credit payments to a minimum. Pay cash for what you can. Get your new car after you've purchased your first property. If credit is an issue, have faith. I'm going to talk about other ways besides a loan from the bank that you can get started investing.

To get a loan, you're also going to need a down payment. The down payment will need to be between 20 and 30 percent of the purchase price. Plan on investing at a minimum $20-30,000 to start.

You don't have to figure out where the down payment is going to come from right at this second and you don't need to start looking up mortgage people. I put this first so that your brain will start processing it in the background. This way these answers will just show up when you need them. Knowing this your brain will start working on what you need to do to be set up for success. You will also feel more empowered when you go to make the call about the loan knowing this information.

One cool side note, if you are currently renting, you can purchase your first investment property pretty easily. The rate will likely be a little bit higher when you tell the bank it's for an investment property. However, that really doesn't matter. What matters most is that the numbers work out to be a good return on your investment. I am okay paying a little bit higher rate if I am still making the return I want, because without the banks money I wouldn't have the opportunity to make more money.

Finding Your Sweet Spot

The second thing you need to do to get started is to identify your sweet spot. All good investors have a sweet spot. Your sweet spot might change, but knowing it will guide your current decisions and keep you grounded. The more grounded you feel in your decisions, the more successful you'll be. What is a sweet spot? It's the area you like to invest in. It's the area you feel comfortable investing in because you know it and you understand it, the nuances work for you.

All sweet spots can be successful. The key to success is liking your sweet spot. In fact, that's the first step of finding your sweet spot. So many people who get started in real estate just pick a property they "think" is going to be good. Maybe it's cheap. Maybe it's in a good neighborhood. Maybe it's been a rental before. There are all kinds of reasons I hear that people think certain properties will be good. Often they're going for the make-money-fast routine instead of seeing themselves as a successful investor.

My first spot, we'll call it semi-sweet spot, happened by default. As I grew as an investor, I've realized what my sweet spot really is. My default investments were half duplexes with garages and yards. They were in a suburb northeast of Denver. I came to know the area really well, because I had three houses there. For me, it was a great place to start, and really paid off.

Now, my sweet spot is small condos very close to the center of Denver. I started making the switch three years ago. At that time it was led by price. I could get into some great places for $50-75,000 that really met my needs. There were a couple things I didn't like about the properties I had, and as I looked there was opportunity to make more money for what felt like less work in the areas I now own.

Hint: If it feels better to you, you're going to make more money.

Some investors really hate my sweet spot. They want to own bigger single-family homes. That is good for them, and if they stick with their sweet spot they will be successful. For me, I *love* my sweet spot, which is why it works so well for me. Your sweet spot guides decisions and reinforces those decisions if you ever question what you're doing.

How do you identify your sweet spot? Ask yourself, who do you want your tenants to be? What areas do you think would be successful for rentals and why? These answers don't have to be perfect. You can reevaluate them later. Who do you want to be living in your investment and why? What area excites you when you say, "I own an investment here (fill in the area)." Let these answers percolate. Later, I'll show you how to evaluate them, and then you can revisit if they still feel like your sweet spot. Your sweet spot is something that is hard to describe in writing, so I've recorded an audio for you that guides you in the process of finding your sweet spot. You can get that here liveyourchampagnelife.com/investing-gifts.

Creating A Team

While your sweet spot is brewing, let's talk about the first members you're going to want to draft to your team. The first one is a good insurance agent. You might find it interesting that an insurance agent is first on your list to put on your team. They're important, because the cost of insurance can often make or break an investment.

Insurance Agent

Your agent needs to be responsive, quick and reliable. After the first investment you make, where you iron out what you desire in a policy, you should be able to send your agent an email telling them about a property you're interested in, and they should send you an estimated quote within 24-48 hours. The cost of insurance is the one piece of information you can estimate on your own, but you really need an agent to give you the solid answer.

I prefer insurance agents who are brokers, and don't just work for one company. This way they can search and get you the best price and coverage, because they aren't locked into one company. The amount you pay for insurance can really impact the return on your investment and it's one of the things you have some control over. On one property, switching insurance companies not only gave me better coverage, but it also increased the rate of return on my money by 1.5% overall.

An insurance agent comes before your real estate agent only because you can get all the information you need for a property to preliminarily evaluate it without a real estate agent. You need your real estate agent to show you the property and to negotiate with the seller's agent, but you want to run your numbers before going to see a property. I love looking at properties. When I do it for fun, it's for fun. But if I'm in business mode, I don't want to be looking at places that won't serve as really good investments.

Real Estate Agent

How do you pick a good real estate agent? The key is to know what you want. Take a few minutes and think about what you desire in an agent. The must haves are quick to respond, someone who understands your vision, someone you trust, someone who makes it feel very comfortable to say no, and most importantly someone you feel will hold your best interest as their highest priority.

An agent needs to be quick to respond, because properties go fast. As an investor, you want to be making moves when the right property comes up. Part of that is on you to have what you need in place, but you have to have an agent who is available and ready when you are. You don't want an agent that is sitting around waiting for you to call. You want him or her to be busy, but have time for you.

One way to determine this is to ask your agent what their goals are. The bigger their goal, the bigger chance they are going to respond to you right away. Communicate your plan of being a long-term investor to them. If they're a good agent, they'll recognize the importance of you as a client, because they're going to get multiple sales from you. If they're not treating you as such, cut them loose as soon as possible.

Go with your gut when it comes to your realtor. You can realtor shop by going to open houses. This gives you a chance to talk to the agent, and get a feel for them. Another way to find a good realtor is to ask around. Get referrals from people you know, like and trust.

I met my current realtor at an open house. I told him I already had a realtor, which I did. He respected that, and still gave me excellent service as he showed me the house. He took a great interest in my business as an investor. I could tell he understood what I was doing, and believed in what I was doing.

A few months after we met, he sent me a property that he came across that he thought I might be interested in. If you ask him, he was just being of service. I attempted to buy that property, but it didn't work out. However, we stayed in touch, and eventually I realized he was more suited for my team than my current realtor. Investing is a business, and you have to be willing to trade your teammates if the current ones aren't supporting your goals.

Brandon, my realtor, meets all of the musts of a realtor. He has big goals. In fact, he's taken some of my courses to increase his money mindset. I always wanted a realtor who understood the power of the right mindset. He wants to sell houses, so he makes time for me when I want to see houses. He understands my long-term goal. He always works for my best interest before he works for his own. He's honest when he doesn't think something fits into my plan. All these things are important and a must in a realtor, but the number one reason he's on my team is because we have a great time together. He loves what he does. He loves helping me invest in properties that make sense, and we entertain each other along the way.

Property Management

The next team member to think about is a property management firm. You don't have to decide whether you want a property manager on your team right now, but the investment in this service is going to make a difference in your bottom line. It's a good idea to think about whether or not you're going to manage your own property or if you'd rather have a property management firm do it for you.

Property management companies can either do everything for you, or can simply place a tenant for you. Everything includes finding the tenant, screening them, getting the deposit, moving them in and out and collecting rent every month. It also includes the day-to-day management. So, if something breaks, they coordinate the people to fix it. They also handle things like evictions, if that's necessary.

The average monthly investment in this full-service is about 10% of the rent. If you don't mind handling the things that come up once in awhile, you can opt for the second kind of service, which is just paying the management company to get you a tenant into your place, and then you take over the rest. This can range from 50-100% of a month's rent. If making the money from real estate appeals to you, but the rest doesn't, definitely consider hiring a property manager.

Hiring a property manager if you're just starting out is a *very* good idea. Until recently, I always hired someone to screen and rent my properties. Hiring someone else at first allows you to learn while having someone else handle things. It keeps you from having to do all the little things that can feel overwhelming when you don't know what you're doing. If at some point you want to take over the management of your properties, the option is always there. I'll talk more in the mindset chapter about how investing in support can grow your investments faster.

Start making a list of who you want on your team. Describe them. Describe their personality, how successful they are, and how they will support your business. As you do this, people already in your life might come to mind. Start making a list of possibilities for your team and of the openings you have for your team. After you've identified who you want to be playing with, start putting your feelers out and start hanging out with other investors. Trust the perfect people will show up.

Quick Review of What You Need to Get Started:

☐ Determine your why

☐ Mortgage Broker/Loan

☐ Down payment 20-30%

☐ Identify your sweet spot

☐ Insurance Agent

☐ Real Estate Agent/Realtor

☐ Property Management Firm

Below is a list of action steps you may want to take:

- Write out your why in a paragraph.
- Listen to the finding your sweet spot recording and start defining your sweet spot
- Find a realtor to interview
- Look up property management firms in your area

Below is a visual overview of the process of investing in real estate to help you start to understand how the process works from start to finish.

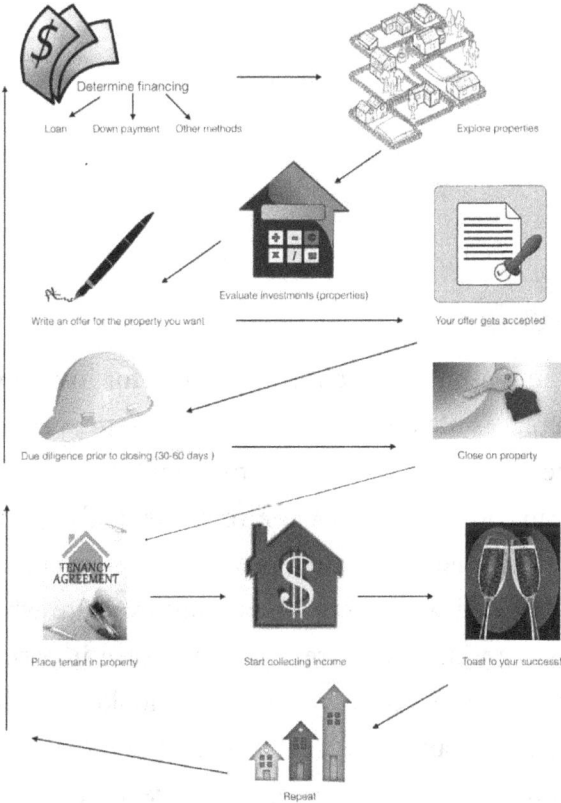

Determine financing

Loan   Down payment   Other methods

Explore properties

Evaluate investments (properties)

Write an offer for the property you want

Your offer gets accepted

Due diligence prior to closing (30-60 days)

Close on property

TENANCY AGREEMENT

Place tenant in property

Start collecting income

Toast to your success!

Repeat

CHAPTER 4
HOW TO EVALUATE
AN INVESTMENT

One reason you identify your *why* for investing in real estate is so that you know how to evaluate the investment. If you're investing for the long term, 30-year payout for retirement, then you simply need to add up all the expenses associated with the property and evaluate what you can charge for rent to make sure it covers the expenses. In this case, you're looking at the long term and your goal is to get the investment paid off, so you can enjoy more of the rent you're collecting.

If you're investing for appreciation, you might want to contact your psychic, because you're playing a guessing game. I'm sure there are some programs out there to help evaluate these opportunities, if this is the type of investing you're interested in.

If you've decided to invest in real estate to get a better return on your investment or for cash flow, I'll walk you through how to evaluate a potential investment. There is more than one way to do everything. I'm going to give you my quick and easy method first. Then I'll give you a more technical formula. I like easy. I also like to evaluate conservatively. The first thing you need to do to evaluate a property is to identify the expenses. Here's a list below:

Identify Expenses

Payment: if you're getting a loan, this is the amount you're paying the bank each month. One of the reasons I suggest investigating the loan first, is that then you have a better idea of how to calculate the payment. When you know about what you'll get for an interest rate and the amount you'll have to put down, you can pull up a mortgage calculator in Excel or Numbers or search online for one to get a good estimate of what you will need to plan on in terms of payments.

Home Owner's Association (HOA) and HOA Dues: Each Home Owner's association charges a monthly fee to all owners. These are fees paid to the Home Owner's Association that cover any number of expenses. If you're looking to purchase a condo or townhouse community, these fees will cover the management company, maintenance to the building, insurance from the drywall in (drywall in is a term used to indicate the HOA is responsible for everything inside the wall up to the drywall), any amenities such as a pool, workout room, roof top deck, trash, water, usually the heat, etc. In a single-family community, the HOA fee usually covers the board and management company. It covers the upkeep of any amenities like a pool, walking paths, clubhouse or green space.

HOA dues vary a lot, and sometimes for no reason you can identify. In condo buildings, a higher HOA fee can be the result of years where the property wasn't properly managed or residents were undercharging, so now the association has to make up for it. For example, in Denver, a fee can vary from $125-300/month for a studio. The monthly HOA fee is something that never goes away. You can't pay it off like a loan. It can also drastically change the economics of an investment. It's important to evaluate the HOA fee. It's important to know exactly what the HOA covers. If there are a lot of amenities that you can charge higher rent for, it might be worth it.

When evaluating a property, you also want to make sure the HOA is financially stable. Ensure they have good financial records (you'll get these during the purchasing process) and they have a reserve. The reserve ensures that they won't require a special assessment. A special assessment is an additional amount each owner is responsible for paying to cover any major expense the HOA didn't have the funds in reserve to cover. Your realtor can help you evaluate the HOA financials.

As you learn your sweet spot, you'll be able to look at the HOA fee and instantly know if this property has the potential to be a good investment. For example, in my sweet spot, I know if the HOA dues are over $130 a month for a one bedroom, it's not going to work as an investment property.

Taxes: Property taxes are set by the state. They vary state to state. In Texas, there is no state tax, so property taxes are higher. If you're using an online system to search for properties, the taxes will be listed in the data online.

Insurance: This is property insurance. Even if the HOA has insurance coverage, you will need additional coverage. HOA insurance coverage generally covers from the drywall in. You need a policy to cover drywall out. Drywall out means everything from the drywall out, which would be the drywall, texture paint, carpet, cabinets, personal belongings etc. This is typically inexpensive, but it's very necessary.

Hint: Make sure to tell your insurance agent that you want a policy that covers the HOA deductible in the event, something in your property causes there to be a claim on the HOA's policy. An HOA can have a $10,000 deductible and they may be able to charge you the deductible. Having it in your insurance policy that the HOA deductible is covered is a really inexpensive way to protect yourself from a big expense.

Property Management: If you are going to enlist the support of a property management company, you will want to include their cost when you figure expenses.

Estimated expenses: There are a lot of ways to estimate expenses. To make it easy, the formula I use is the expected rent and 11 months (I assume one month is going to go for maintenance or to cover the place being empty for a few days) and then I divide it by 12. Note: When you get to the point of buying multi-units the bank will evaluate using a vacancy rate. A good estimate for a vacancy rate is 3% and a good estimate for maintenance is 7%. As time goes on you'll identify a quick and easy method for you.

Other Information To Identify:
Estimated Rent: What can you charge for rent? It's important to be conservative and close to right on this one. If you want to get a feel for property management companies, call and see if

they'll do a rent estimate for free. If they won't, I would cross them off the list. There are a lot of tools you can use to evaluate rent. Personally, I use padmapper.com when I'm first starting out. Other good tools are rentometer.com and zillow.com. (These are also listed on the resources page at the end of the book.) When you're first starting out it's good to compare sites. The tools to evaluate rent can vary by area, so I would search online to find one you like, if these don't work for your area. There is also a resources guide at the back of the book.

A great way to figure out how to evaluate rent is to ask someone you know who would be looking for a place to rent. Ask them what service they would use. If you decide to add a Property Management company to your team, they should send you their estimates for any place you are looking at purchasing. If they don't do this free of charge as a courtesy service, I would investigate other companies. The reason I would investigate others is if they won't provide it for free, they might not be too interested in your business. It's an easy process for a management company because a) they do it all the time and b) they generally pay for advanced tools. If they're looking for your business they should be more than willing to share something that takes them five to ten minutes to evaluate.

Purchase Price: The total amount paid for the investment. This is the amount you paid at closing. It's the total of any closing costs, the purchase price, etc.

Investment Out of Pocket: This amount includes your down payment and any other money you invested to get the property ready to rent.

Cassie's Evaluation Process

Here's an example evaluation using one of my properties:

PURCHASE PRICE: $52,000
Monthly:

Payment:	$183
HOA:	$125
Taxes:	$25
Insurance:	$15
Total:	$348

Rent:	$725
Investment Out of Pocket (down payment and fix up):	$21,000
Annual Rent (11 months) :	$7975
Annual Known Expenses :	$4176
Annual Net:	$3799
ROI (return on investment):	18%

Step by step

- Add up the payment, HOA, taxes and insurance. Then multiply the total by 12 to get your annual expenses.
- $183+$125+$25+$15=$348 x 12 =$4,176
- Multiply the rent by 11 to get your estimated annual rent.
- $725x11=$7975
- Subtract your annual expense from your estimated annual rent. This is your estimated annual profit.
- $7975-$4176=$3799
- Divide your estimated annual profit by your investment out of pocket (down payment + any renovations that were done). This equals your estimated ROI, return on investment.
- $3799/$21,000=18%

In the example above, the ROI is 18%. When I worked for a financial services company, it was considered an extremely successful investment if a mutual fund performed at an average of 12%. In my experience, most mutual funds don't average 12%. By investing in real estate, I set myself up for a return on my money that I like, and if I'm not going to get what I want as a return, I don't invest.

I am ultra conservative so I play the "what if" game a lot. It's not helpful for some people, but I like to get comfortable with all possibilities. When I purchased this investment, I didn't know about all the rent tools available. One of my "what ifs" was only being able to get $600 rent. I knew if I could only get that I would still make over 11% on this investment.

The even better news? Someone else is paying off the mortgage for me, so if and when I want to sell it, I will owe less than I paid. I also get the bonus of appreciation on the property. On this property, it's a very good bonus.

I made this investment when the market was low in Denver. If I were to purchase this property today, would it still be a good investment?

ESTIMATED PURCHASE PRICE: $115,000

Investment Out of Pocket
(25% down payment): $28,750

Monthly:

Payment:	$437
HOA:	$125
Taxes:	$25
Insurance:	$15
Total:	$602
Rent:	$825
Investment (down payment):	$28,750
Annual Rent (11 months):	$9,075
Annual Expenses:	$7,224
Annual Net:	$1,851
ROI (return on investment):	6.6%

I would prefer to be making 10% straight out on the cash I put down, but in this case, the market is in an upswing. If I was purchasing right now, I'd consider properties like this because here's another factor to consider, approximately $100 a month the first year is going to pay down what you owe on the mortgage. If you add $1200 to the Annual Net of $1851 that totals $3051 and that is about an 11%

return on the investment. It doesn't earn cash flow returns at 11%, but when you look at all factors, it's greater than a 10% return. The other cool thing is because of the way interest is calculated on a mortgage each year, more and more of the principal is being paid off. This means that the ROI gets better every year. In a few years, the ROI will likely be greater than 12%.

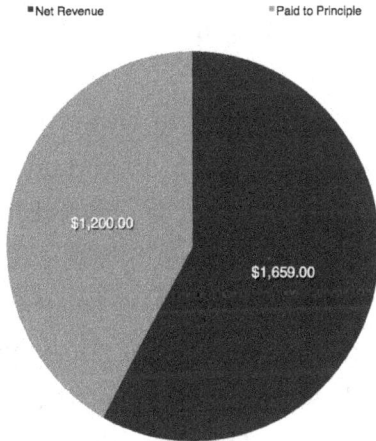

In a situation like this, you want to plan on holding your property for a few years. A realtor can help you do the math to see what the actual return on your investment will be after you've owned this investment for 5 or more years.

That's where the numbers get more fun and exciting.

There are so many factors to consider when investing in real estate. That's why it's necessary to have a realtor who really understands investment properties. They can help you get a much clearer picture of the returns that are likely from a potential investment. For me, I was fortunate to grab this property when prices were down. However, it still makes sense now, if I have the money and the time is right for me to invest.

Real estate is likely to always have its ups and downs. It's more important that the investment makes sense, as opposed to whether the market is up or down. It's true, if you buy when the market is high, your property could at some point be worth less than you paid, however if you're still collecting rent, and someone else is paying down the principal, does it matter? The market usually comes back up. A property I paid $160,000 for, dropped at its lowest to about $115,000 and I sold it six months ago for $195,000. The key is, it was making money the whole time it was an investment.

If you walk into a realtor's office and tell them you're looking to make 10% or more on the money you invest, or tell them you're using Cassie's method, they might not understand what you're talking about – so I'm going to give you some insight on the industry speak so you can feel more confident. Keep in mind, I successfully retired from my job on my passive income from real estate, and didn't learn what I'm about to tell you until about six months ago. I tell you that so you know you don't *have* to know everything to get started. You just have to get started and do what makes sense to you and is in alignment with your goals and intentions.

Real Estate Industry Evaluation

In the Real Estate industry, they call your return on investment the Cap rate. The Cap rate is what determines whether something is a good investment or not. The Cap rate is calculated by taking the Net Operating Income (rental income minus the net operating expenses) and dividing that by the purchase price. The Cap rate should be between 6-8%. Generally speaking, the lower the Cap rate, the easier the investment is to manage and the higher the Cap rate the more potential headaches. It's not a guarantee, it's just the way income properties are listed and evaluated.

In the example above, the Cap rate would be just over 6% with a purchase price of $115,000.

Annual Rent	
($825 x.9=742.50 x 12):	$8910
Annual Expenses (HOA, Taxes and Insurance) excluding the payment:	$1980
Net Operating Income (Rent-Expenses):	$6930
At a 6% Cap rate ($6930/.06) purchase price:	$115,500
At a 7% Cap rate ($6930/.07) purchase price:	$99,000
At an 8% Cap rate ($6930/.08) purchase price:	$86,625

What does this mean? If you're purchasing a property that is being sold as an investment, they should use this formula to determine the price. In the case of the property we're talking about, it's in a great location and it's really easy to rent. There's very little maintenance, so it would make sense for it to be at a 6% Cap rate if it was being sold as an investment property. This property would likely sell to an owner occupant for more than $115,000, so it might not be a viable investment option for someone who wants a greater than 6% Cap rate.

The second number used in the real estate industry to evaluate rate of return is called the Internal Rate of Return. This includes a lot of calculations and is better explained by your realtor. This number that is going to show you how much you're making takes into account the principle on the mortgage that's being paid. A good Internal Rate of Return is around 15%, and really experienced investors can average 24%. The longer you do something the more you learn and the better you get at it. Starting with a 15% Internal Rate of Return is a really good rate of return. With intention and as you get better you'll learn how to move towards the 24%.

A good realtor can sit down with actual properties and explain these numbers and calculations to you. If you are getting started, I would highly recommend finding a realtor that understands investments and how to do these calculations or at least is willing to learn. My current realtor invited me to a class where I learned all this stuff along side him. As I said, I was successful without knowing a lot of this. However, I want you to walk into a realtor's office confident that you have an idea of what's going on.

When you do walk into a realtor's office, interview them. It's okay not to know. You're new. Evaluate them based on the time they take to walk you through things. They will likely ask what Cap rate and Internal Rate of Return you're looking for. This is how they prequalify you. If you walk in and say a 20 Cap rate, and they know what they're doing, they're probably going to refer you to someone else because they know that's unreasonable. Prepare yourself, think of what you're looking to make and then go in with a list of questions you'd like answered.

Below is an action step you may want to take:

- Create a spreadsheet or worksheet to keep track of and calculate expenses and rent.

CHAPTER 5
HOW TO GET STARTED IF YOU DON'T HAVE A DOWN PAYMENT

You just read how to evaluate a property, which is really exciting because you can start getting awesome returns! But what if you don't have $20,000-30,000 in cash right now to get started? I'm going let you in on a little secret: the key to getting started is to start. Sounds weird, right? What I am talking about is making a decision, setting an intention that you're going to invest, and then taking a small action step that moves your energy in that direction. I'm going to give you a list of ways you can get started in real estate right now. Take one action step on one of them to really get the ball rolling.

You're a smart woman, so I'm guessing you are taking advantage of your 401(k) plan at your place of employment. If you're not, meet me below for a little pow wow to talk about why you might want to.

Hint: If you are fortunate to work somewhere that matches your 401(k) contributions, and you're not taking advantage of it, you're walking away from free money. Even if you don't plan on being there long enough to get vested, you might end up being there long enough after all, and then you can't go back in time and change it. If you don't like the investments they offer, or you're afraid the market is going down, invest in the most conservative thing offered or contact the person in charge for advice. This way you can collect the extra money the company has to give you as a match to your contribution. It's free money!

401(k) Loan Option

You have a 401(k) at work. Almost all 401(k) plans have a loan option. Yes, they charge an interest rate, but that interest gets paid back to you. Additionally, there is no approval based on credit. If you want the loan, you can take it as long as your account meets the guidelines. The loan terms are usually 5 years or less, but think of what you can do in 5 years? Depending on how much you have in your 401(k) you could come up with a nice down payment or possibly even pay for an entire property with a loan from your 401(k).

Hint: If you pay cash for a property and establish yourself as an investor (if you haven't been one before) and demonstrate that the investment makes money, you might be able to get a Home Equity Line of Credit (HELOC) from the bank with very little effort.

What does this secret mean to you? You can possibly buy a property with cash (outright with no loan) with your 401K loan. If you were able to get a loan from the bank after you've purchased the property using your 401K loan they would likely give you a loan for 60% of the value. You would then pay that 60% back over 30 years, and likely at a lower interest rate, so it would be a much smaller payment. You could then pay the amount you were loaned from the bank back to your 401K loan, thus owing less of a payment each month to your 401K.

You can see how you can use your 401K to get started, and then leverage a mortgage to get your payment lower. In this scenario, it might cost you more money out of pocket up front than you're making, but depending on your *why* and your situation, it might make sense. You have to determine that for yourself, based on your goals and the additional amount you desire to invest in your financial future.

If you don't have 100K in your 401(k) right now, or you don't think you can get a property for 100K, don't worry about it. I'm giving you all this information so that when you get started, your brain will have all this info stored away. Then when you go to figure things out, all these possibilities will be available to your creativity.

Are there reasons you have to be cautious using your 401(k) for loans? Yes, use your common sense with everything you do. Investigate. If you're interested in a 401(k) loan, talk to your 401(k) company and/or your Human Resources contact. There are things you need to know before you take a 401(k) loan, but if you know why you're doing it, you can easily evaluate if it's the right move for you.

Here's a hypothetical from my own life. The property that I gave as an example above, which I call Marion, was $52,000. In order to get a mortgage on it, I had to put down 30%, which made the loan I needed to take $36,400. For that loan, the bank was going to charge me $5,000 because it was such a small mortgage. I was only willing to pay over 10% for a loan if I had to.

Below is a hypothetical example of the above paragraph.

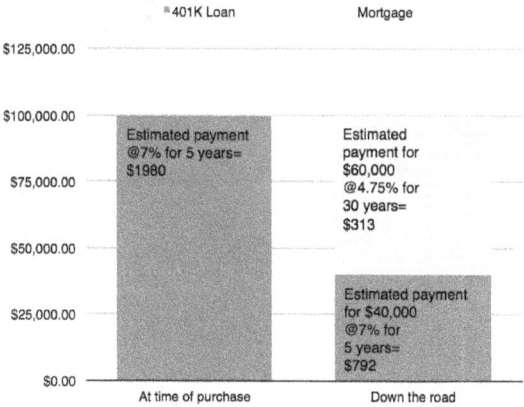

This is when I investigated taking a loan from my 401K to purchase this investment. I ended up taking an equity loan on another property to purchase this one, but had I had to take a 401(k) loan I would have. Next I'm going to walk you through a hypothetical 401(k) loan because there's magic in the power of this type of loan. You'll see how taking a 5 year loan from your 401(k) can lead to having an investment that you own outright, while paying yourself 7% interest. However, if you don't have a 401(k), or are not interested in taking a loan from it, you can skip to the next section.

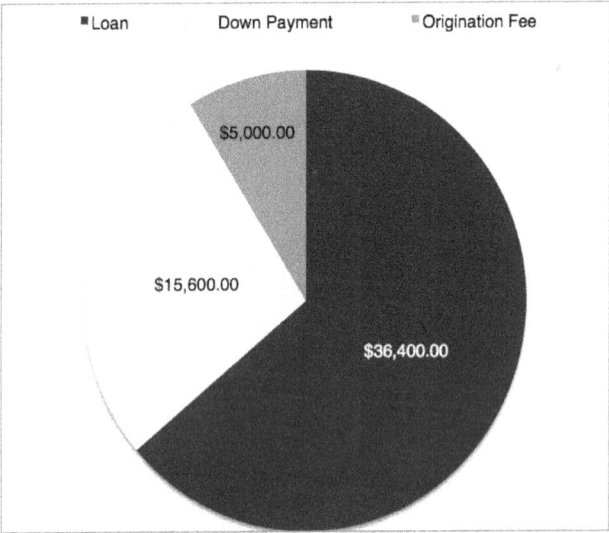

I had $17,000 to put down so the loan would have been $35,000 to be paid back over 5 years with a payment of approximately $624 a month. The other expenses on this house are $175. The total is $800 a month. At the time, it rented for

$725 a month. Which means it would have cost me $75 out of my pocket each month to purchase the property.

At first, that doesn't seem like a great idea, since my intention is to earn more than 10% on my investments (in this case $17,000). However, had I done that, that property would have been free and clear in 5 years. It now rents for $825 a month. Had I taken the 401(k) loan, 2-1/2 years later, the rent would be covering the full payment, and it's now worth $115,000. I could get a Home Equity Loan on it for about $19,000 (which is what I would still owe on the 401(k) loan) and the payment would be about $100. In this scenario, I would be making about $550 profit a month, which is well over a 20% ROI on the investment I made ($17,000 down and $100/month for 30 months).

If I were to just continue paying off the 401(k) loan, and paid it off 2-1/2 years from now, I would be making more than a 25% ROI on my total investment on a monthly basis. By total investment, I mean money I actually paid toward the investment out of my pocket. I would be making 25%, have a passive income of approximately $6500 a year, and own a property that is worth $115,000 outright. The math might be challenging to follow, but what is easy to follow is that it would have been a very good use of my 401(k) because in addition to all the value from the property, I was paying the loan back to myself at 7% interest.

There would have been no way to predict that property would now be worth $115,000. I could have hoped and crossed my fingers but I couldn't have known or sure. The point is, the investment made sense without factoring in appreciation. And it really makes sense *with* appreciation. I always see appreciation as a bonus. Even if the property were still only worth $52,000, it would have been a very smart investment. And taking a loan from my 401(k) in order to get started totally would have made sense. In this case, there would have been some out-of-pocket money, but it would have paid off big.

In this case, it would take 5 years to see the cash flow, but it's worth it because at the end of 5 years, there's a great investment with great cash flow, a huge return on money invested, and a property that is free and clear. At this point, I would get a Home Equity Loan to have available for future down payments to purchase additional properties.

Are there issues that could arise from taking a 401(k) loan? Of course, but the better you understand them up front, the better off you'll be. Educate yourself. Read the loan information and talk to your accountant. If you leave your job for any reason you'll have to pay the remainder of the loan back in a certain time period or you have to pay taxes on it. In this case if you were far enough into the loan you could probably get a Home Equity Loan or you might be able to get a personal line of credit with the house as collateral. That would give you the ability to pay back the 401(k) loan and not incur any taxes.

You might decide to just have the investment paid off, by not paying back the loan, and paying the taxes. In the case above, one year's profit (without a payment) may be enough to cover the taxes. Everyone's situation is going to be unique, so you want to discuss your options with your tax accountant.

The most important thing is to be aware up front. Understanding the "what ifs" up front will give you more confidence going in. Being prepared mentally for the "what ifs" will also keep you from operating out of desperation if one of those "what ifs" happens to be true. The "what ifs" are the things you learn as you investigate the loan. An example, is what if you lose your job, or quit your job, while you have the loan? How will you handle the taxes? Or what if the property rents for $50-100 less than you expected? Will you have enough on a monthly basis to cover that without causing financial stress? What if you go a month without getting rent? Can you make the payment on the loan? All these are "what ifs" to plan out prior to getting an investment. The more informed and comfortable you are up front, the more success you will experience.

In my case, I left my job what would have been a year into this loan. I had the money to pay off the loan when I left, so I might have done that. Or it would have cost me about $8400 in taxes in order to keep the money and not pay off the loan. If I choose to pay the taxes and keep the money, the ROI would be about 12%. That's awesome!

Utilizing A 401K From A Former Job

Taking a loan is a great way to utilize your current 401K. What about those old 401Ks or other retirement vessels you have from jobs you no longer work at? Once you decide on your investment strategy, you might want to consider cashing one, two or five of those out and investing in real estate.

What about the taxes? There's really no way around it, if you take money out of a retirement investment, you're going to have to pay taxes. My mom always says, "You're at the lowest tax bracket you're ever going to be right now." She says that to 20 year olds and 40 year olds. My mom holds the intention for everyone that their income grows with their age. What my mom is saying, and it's good advice, is that if you're going to pay taxes on a 401K or something similar, you might as well do it sooner rather than later. If your intention is to make a bigger and bigger salary, or make more and more in your business, then you should do it sooner rather than later. It doesn't make sense to skip doing something that has the outcome you desire, just because you might have to pay some extra taxes.

No one wants to pay taxes, especially extra taxes, but it's part of the game. Is it worth holding yourself back from making a better return on your money because you'll have to pay a tax penalty upfront? That's a personal decision everyone has to make. For me, the answer is *hell no*. I would rather be in control of my money and making investments in real estate that make sense to me based on the ROIs I desire. It's worth it to me to pay some taxes and be reaching my goals. If your *why* is a better return on your money, and you're not as concerned with cash flow, a self-directed IRA (discussed below) might be a better option.

I have a 401(k) that is sitting and waiting for the right property to come along. My 401(k) has had its best year in a long time, and it only made 10%. For me, it makes complete sense to leverage that money to make more. I'm in the process of finding a multi-unit building that I can invest in with my 401(k). This makes sense for me, because I am investing for cash flow.

The keys to investing with your 401(k) are being informed, and knowing your *why*. Last year, there was an investment I wanted to purchase and I was going to utilize my 401(k) to purchase the property. I believe in being informed, so I called the 1-800 number for my 401(k). The nicest man picked up the phone and answered all my questions. In the middle of the conversation, he said, "Well, we always recommend that you don't cash out a retirement account, but since you're already retired, it seems like you know what you're doing."

You're trained by the 401(k) industry and the people around you that you should never cash out a 401(k). I'm a smart, savvy, financially intelligent woman. I agree there are a lot of reasons not to cash out your 401(k). A trip to the Bahamas is one of them. However, my goal has always been to retire comfortably. I believe in making sound financial choices that support *my* financial goals. When the right opportunity presents itself to invest in a property rather than leave my money in my 401(k), I'm taking it. I'm patient. It has to be the right opportunity. The numbers have to make sense.

I highly recommend you utilize the 1-800 number or your Human Resources department. There are reasons to roll your 401(k) over to an IRA if you're going to use it for an investment. The reasons can change, which is why you want to keep yourself informed. When I did it, it's because you can take some out of your IRA and you don't have to take it all. Under the rules of the 401K plan I had, I would have had to take all of it. There's another reason I'm going to talk about as well.

Utilizing Your IRA For 60 Days

Ask as many questions as you want. It's by asking questions that I learned this super secret, unofficial way to use your IRA. Let me tell you first what most people don't know. You can take a withdrawal from your IRA, and if you pay it back within 60 days (it has to be on or before the 60th day), you don't have to pay taxes on it. And you can do this once every rolling twelve months. You can confirm this by talking to your IRA administrator.

Why is this so cool? If you want to purchase a property, but for some reason you can't get the loan, this is an alternative. There's a variety of reasons traditional lending may not be available: you're not an experienced investor, the mortgage process can be difficult on investment properties sometimes, etc. You can use this IRA rule to help create a way to get the investment property. Let's say you purchase the property cash (meaning you don't take out any mortgage for it) utilizing the funds from your IRA. If you can get it rented, and show income, you can then go to the bank and apply for a Home Equity Loan. In my experience, Home Equity Loans are quick. There's not a lot of paperwork, and many of the the hoops that you have to jump through when you're getting a first mortgage don't exist in the Home Equity Loan process.

To give you an example, I've been self-employed for a little over a year. I don't have a long enough income record as a self-employed person to qualify for a traditional loan. However, I was able to easily get a Home Equity Loan on one of my properties that is paid off. The turn around time, if I was in town and on my game, would have been about two weeks. That's very fast. This is for a loan to value (how much the house is worth compared to the loan amount) of 60%.

In the case of using your IRA (which you can roll a 401(k) over into upon leaving a job), you could purchase the property cash, rent it and then take out a loan to pay 60% of the money back. Going this route, you'll only have to pay taxes on the 40% that you're not paying back immediately. This is a great way to utilize your IRA to get into an investment if you can't or don't want to get a traditional mortgage.

Hint: Down the road, you might want to look at refinancing the Home Equity Loan. Most home equity loans' interest rates are based on prime, which can change. By refinancing into a fixed rate loan, you'll protect yourself from the possibility of a rising interest rate.

This is also a great solution if you want to invest in real estate, but have a really large IRA, so the tax hit would be significant if taken all at once. Imagine if you purchased one investment a year. You'd slowly move your IRA into investment properties, and you would spread the tax hit out over a few years, which would actually reduce the total amount of taxes you would have to pay to take the money out. This little secret gives you a lot of power and opportunity.

Remember, when you're ready to do it, give the 1-800 number a call to confirm you fully understand how the process works, and what you need to do to successfully return the funds.

You will also want to investigate the loan situation first. Feel out if there would be any obstacles in getting the Home Equity Loan. Be prepared for the "what ifs." If for some reason the loan doesn't work, make sure you can pay the taxes. Set yourself up for success by knowing what you need to do and having contingency plans in case your original plan takes a detour.

Self-Directed IRA

Taking a tax hit, or a possible tax hit might make sense if you're investing for cash flow and setting yourself up to leave your job. However, if you're investing for a better rate of return over the long term, and you want to utilize your IRA, you can set up a self-directed IRA. This way you can take advantage of better rates of return and you will not have to pay any taxes because you are not taking out your retirement money. You are simply using it in a different type of investment.

Purchase A House To Live In, Convert To An Investment

What if you don't currently have a 401(k), or you're not ready to jump in and use your 401(k) as a tool? You can always purchase a house for yourself and live there for 6 to 12 months, and then move out and convert it to an investment property. Getting into a house as an owner occupant can be easier than purchasing an investment property straight away. The down payment can be as little as 3% of the purchase price, which means there can be little that you have to put down out of pocket. This is a great way to get started, if you don't have the cash for a larger down payment. If you go this route, make sure the rent you will get in the future is enough to cover the payment and estimated expenses.

Utilizing The Equity In Your House

Maybe you already own a house, and you're not ready to move out of it yet. Depending on the market, you could take the equity out of your current house and use it for a down payment on an investment property. This option takes some analysis to figure out if it makes sense. Run all the numbers on the potential investment to ensure it's a good decision to take equity out of your house and invest it elsewhere. Prior to doing this, I would also suggest setting up a savings account that has enough in it to cover both payments for a couple months, just in case. There will be more about this in the mindset section.

Start Saving For A Down Payment

A really great option for creating the money for a down payment is to start a savings fund for it. If you get bonuses at work, you can commit those to getting started in real estate investing. Put your tax return in a fund each year that is savings for the down payment on an investment property. Once you commit money to saving for a down payment, more money will show up. All you have to do is start the process.

Maybe you don't get bonuses or tax refunds. You can still start a savings account that is for real estate investing. Commit an amount of money you can invest in your future investment each month. You might be thinking, *I can only save a couple hundred a month. That's not going to get me to $20,000 for a down payment.* Again, setting the intention and getting the process started is the most important thing. If you don't start today, next year you'll be even further from your goal.

Once you start saving, the amount you have for real estate investing will snowball. For example, if you committed to saving $250 a month, that would be $3000 a year. If you did that for seven years, you would have $21,000 to invest. Fabulous, you purchase your first property. Now you're making an extra $2,100 a year (10% return on your investment). If you add that to the $3000, you are already saving per year, in approximately four years, you'll have another $21,000 to invest in another property.

If you continue the process, and add the additional $2,100 to the $5,100 a year that you're saving, you will have another down payment in 3 years. And then just 2 years later you can purchase another one.

Now, it's 15 years later, you have four properties, and are making approximately $8400 a year. You're now saving $11,400 a year, which means you can purchase a new property every two years.

Twenty years in, you have six properties and about $12,000 of passive income coming in each year. That's $1,000 a month. If you started when you were 35, you would now be 55. What could you do with an extra $1000 a month when you're 55? Go on cool trips? Pay for your kids college? Quit your full time job and get a part time job?

In this scenario, we're only talking about cash flow. In addition to cash flow, your first purchase is only ten years away from being paid off, and is likely worth much more than you paid for it. In ten years, when you're 65, you'll have $1,000 in addition to the full rent on your first place to supplement your income. Additionally, you'll have equity in all of your investments (because the mortgage has been paid down) which means you could sell a couple of them and pay off the others, and have even more income each month.

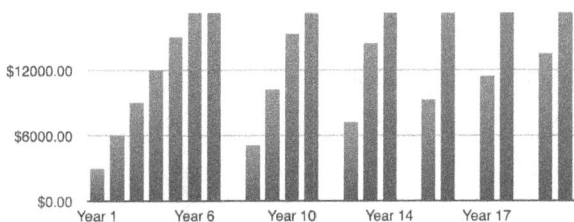

Imagine if you continued the process until you are 65. You could purchase 6 more properties and your monthly income would be almost $2,000 a month, which might not sound like a lot, but what if your house was paid off? And if you paid off half of the properties with the equity from the others, you'd have close to another $2,000 a month coming in. The properties are going to be worth much more than you paid for them, so you'd likely have a big stack of cash as well. All of this for a $90,000 investment ($250/month for 30 years).

Plugging the above scenario into a retirement calculator at CNN.com, if you are 35 and you want to retire at 65, you need to be saving 15% of your income, which is $7,200 a year if you want to retire with an income of $48,000 a year. $48,000 is the same amount of income we created by saving $250 a month or $3000 a year and investing it in real estate. All of this is hypothetical, of course. But when I compare hypothetical apples to apples, I'm going to go with the scenario that requires me to save $3,000 a year instead of $7,200.

There are so many ways to get started investing in real estate. From 401K loans to saving every month, there are so many possibilities. I've tried to create an easy guide for you to which decision is right for you, but the truth is there are too many factors to consider because each of you is different. Knowing your *why*, identifying your goals and acting from inspiration will lead you to the right path for you. If you get inspired by one of these methods, that's fantastic. If the waters still feel a bit muddy, you don't have to make a decision right now. Focus on your goals and your *why*. Contact a realtor and learn more. Get on the internet and start looking at properties for fun. The answer will reveal itself when you're ready.

Review: Ways To Get Started If You Don't Have a Down Payment

- 401K Loan
- Utilizing a 401K from a former job
- Utilizing an IRA for 60 days
- Self-Directed IRA
- Purchase a house to live in, and turn it into an investment later
- Utilize the equity in your current home
- Start saving for a down payment

CHAPTER 6
HAVING AN INVESTOR'S MINDSET

On occasion, because I enjoy learning as much as I can, I find myself sitting at a conference room table surrounded by people taking a class on real estate investing. The instructor, no matter who it is, starts the class by going around the room and having people introduce themselves by saying their name, whether they're a real estate agent or investor, and sometimes how many properties they own. I've done this routine more than once. As the metaphorical torch gets passed, we all state our name and give ourselves a title. When it's my turn, I introduce myself as an investor.

I know what you call yourself matters, so I sit on the edge of my chair listening to everyone introduce themselves. You can tell what kind of questions or "problems" someone is going to present during the class, based on what they call themselves. About 20 percent of the people who own rental properties will introduce themselves as a landlord. I'm guessing you just had an interesting visual pop into your head. You also might have felt yucky or a little stressed. Maybe you squirmed in your chair a bit.

All of these reactions are the result of what the word landlord means to you, and what you think about being one. Inevitably, everyone who introduced themselves as a landlord, will come up with a question or a story that relates to what they do being hard. People who call themselves "landlord" share stories so interesting you couldn't even make them up. They're filled with drama, and like I said, lots of hard work.

Now then, there's the investors' questions and stories. These are filled with successes of finding an amazing deal. Their stories generally have a good outcome. If their stories involve a bit of drama, they don't come off that way – and at the end there is a lesson they integrated into their business model and have been more successful since.

Calling myself a landlord was never an option because of the squirmy, yucky feeling you experienced when you thought about it. Not wanting to call myself a landlord, I used to say, "I own properties." Better, but not awesome. Something changed when I started calling myself a real estate investor. It rolls off my tongue differently than saying, "I own properties." I stand up straighter when I call myself an investor. I give myself more credit for being smart when I call myself an investor.

Mindset is everything if you're going to become a real estate investor (or whatever glorious name you give yourself). I have a friend whose whole business centers around choosing the label that will activate success. She changed her world by deciding she was a Goddess of Lattes instead of just a barista. Choose your label wisely and with intent, because it is how you tell the world to treat you.

The world treats *investors* very differently than it treats landlords. When I started calling myself an investor, those in my life responded by asking about my success, instead of my problems managing my properties. I have a couple of friends who always joke when we're together about what building I'm going to buy next. I'm guessing if I called myself a landlord we'd be joking about a broken sink instead of replacing the name of a huge corporation on the side of the building with my own.

Decide on your label before you ever start investing in properties, because it will impact your experience. Picking your label is the first step in creating an investor's mindset. The second is deciding what you're going to call your properties. Are they rentals? I choose to call mine investments because that is exactly what they are. They are an investment of my money in my future. I also want them to perform as investments and make me lots of money.

Giving your investment a proper name will also support you in seeing it for what it is. I would say don't get emotionally attached to your properties, and if you can stay totally detached, do it. I have small emotional attachments to many of my properties, because each one of them represents my increased success. I understand myself enough to know

I'm going to get a little attached. The attachment comes up as a minor issue when I decide I want to sell them. It doesn't take too long to work through it. I acknowledge them and thank them for their part in my success and then release them.

Having a small emotional attachment to a place because it represents success or because it was your first investment is okay. You can work through that. However, an investor has to see their properties as investments. This can be challenging if someone damages a place, or doesn't take care of it like you thought they would. That's part of the process. It's going to happen. And you have to find a way to stay neutral and not take the actions of other people personally. It has nothing to do with you.

What do you do if you get frustrated because it doesn't work out the way you wanted, or someone damages a place, or worse yet – isn't paying rent. These are all good reasons to hire a property manager. The property manger will lessen the impact of these things on you. Even if you have a property manager, you're going to have to deal with some of these things.

Decide ahead of time, when you pick your label, how you handle bumps in the road and keep your intentions in mind. When you pick your label, decide how someone with your label is going to handle it if she or he doesn't get a property she wanted. How are you (thinking like your label) going to handle it when it's stressful because something breaks? How are you going to handle it when you can't find a tenant, or you have to fire your property management company, or someone moves out and trashes your place?

Set an intention for everything about investing in real estate to be smooth sailing (meaning everything goes according to plan and is easy), but prepare yourself just in case it doesn't work out that way. Preparing for the situations you don't want to deal with will lessen the chance they happen, because you're not afraid of them. And preparing to handle a worst case scenario sets you up to handle any situation that comes up with ease and grace. For example, if your worst case scenario is that your place doesn't get rented for two months, you plan ahead and have two months' rent in savings dedicated to that property. Then if that worst case happens, you know you can handle it.

The other way to keep yourself in a positive mindset as an investor is to make sure you have a cushion of money, just in case. It can seem like planning to have the money to take care of things that come up would be attracting more of them into your life. How it really works is, if you don't have a cushion and then something happens and you're not prepared, then you end up stressed about money. Whenever you operate in the space of not enough, you attract more "not enough."

As an investor, when you operate from a space of not having enough money, it manifests as one problem that requires money after another. That's because you keep recreating things to demonstrate "there's not enough." However, if you plan and set aside money to take care of incidentals, then you simply pay them and move on. If you don't have money set aside, and something big happens, then you go into panic mode trying to pay for it. This can quickly lead to a downward spiral of stress and money out the window.

When you get stressed about money, you make quick decisions and they originate from the fight/flight/freeze part of your brain. This is the part of your brain that makes survival decisions. When you get stressed, it kicks in. The problem is this part of your brain is attempting to keep you safe, and not make good decisions for the long term.

Your logical part of your brain is best used for long-term decision-making that supports success in investments. The best way to ensure you utilize this part of your brain when making decisions is to reduce amount of stress you experience when it comes to your investments. The less stress, the calmer you remain. You make really good decisions when you're calm, cool and collected.

How do you set yourself up to remain calm, cool and collected? It starts with making good investments. This means you do your homework up top. You evaluate your investment with real numbers. If it's not a good investment, walk away and wait for the right investment to come along. If you start investing in something that doesn't feel solid because you're hoping it will work out or hoping you will be able to get higher rent then you're starting out stressed and desperate. That stress and desperation will follow you the entire time you own that investment.

Make good decisions. Don't spread yourself too thin. Make sure the investment covers all the expenses and a maintenance reserve. Make sure you can cover if there happens to be a month without rent. Then, when you have to spend money, you just roll with it because you accounted for it. All the money you need should be covered by the rent you're collecting. Make sure to keep it separate from your other money, so it's always available.

If you're just starting out, set up a team to support you. It's a very good idea to invest in a property management company, especially if it's your first investment. They will take care of getting your place rented. They will do the background and credit check and get a good lease signed.

The other advantage of a property management company is they have contractors they use all the time. This eliminates the need for you to screen contractors or worse, just pick someone at random. If a contractor works regularly with the management company, they count on them for work, which means they do their best work. The property management company likely gets a volume discount for the amount of work they give to each contractor. The property management company passes this savings on to you.

If you choose not to hire a property management company, make sure you find contractors you trust ahead of time. You want to know you trust their work, before there is an emergency. And you don't want to have to just take the first guy who answers his phone if you need something done right away. And most things having to do with an investment need to be done right away.

Hiring a property manager is likely going to save you money in the end, because of the discount contractors get, and also because they know how to screen tenants and write leases. All of this will take you five times as long, because you don't know how to do it. It could also end up costing you three times as much, if you make a mistake.

In addition to the money, there is the time and energy it takes to manage a property. If you're working a full-time job, you likely don't have a lot of free time – and the free time you do have, you probably want to enjoy instead of spending it managing a property. It also takes energy to handle things that come up in relation to an investment property. Since you'll be learning as you go, it's going to take a lot of energy at first.

Spending a lot of time and energy on an investment is likely to wear on you after a while, and you'll get frustrated and start to resent your investment. All of a sudden it doesn't seem worth it, and you'll be tempted to get out or at the very least not get another investment.

On the other hand, if you hire someone who is really good at what they do, the money will feel so easy. Money flows where there is ease and grace. Therefore, the easier you make your investment on yourself, the more successful you'll be. If after a while you learn what needs to be done and you feel comfortable, take over management. It's always an option, but if you find the right management company, you likely won't want to take it over. You'll be too busy investing in more properties.

Part of becoming a real estate investor is realizing and accepting you're different. Not everyone will invest in real estate for one reason or another. But if you put yourself in the club, if you make the choice to invest, adopt a bad-ass investor attitude.

One of the best things that ever happened to me was starting the eviction process on someone. In the beginning, I would hire a management company to put the tenants in my houses, and then I would take over management. For the most part, I liked this system. I hired someone to do the part I hated doing, and I did what felt easy to me.

Managing the month-to-month stuff was easy. I have a contractor I trust, so if something needed fixing, I just called him and he went and handled it. Other than that, I pretty much just cashed the checks and paid the mortgage. That was – until someone stopped paying rent on time. I gave them chances, and for about six months, they would get caught up and then they wouldn't pay – and they still wouldn't pay by the time we agreed upon.

Eventually, I knew I would have to evict them. Paying a lawyer was more than I wanted to spend. I used my pre-paid legal services and they pointed me to the forms on my county website. I was angry and frustrated, and to be honest, a little scared. This was a big deal. I wasn't sure how I was going to handle it. If you've ever read the eviction process, it's pretty intense.

I put on my big girl pants and went to work. One day, I filled out the forms at lunch. The next day, I drove the 30 minutes to the courthouse – only to wait in line and have to drive 30 minutes back because I hadn't filled something out right. By the time I want back the next day, I had all my Ts crossed. Filing at the court is only the first of many steps.

You have to post a notice on the door, hire a process server, or talk one of your friends into walking the forms up and knocking on the door. Then if they pay, you're safe until the next month, where the whole process starts over again. Eventually, you get far enough along that you go to court – at which point they ask you if you can work something out before you see the judge. That was easy, because my tenant knew they weren't paying. Then you wait again for the day they're supposed to pay.

When that day comes, they beg and plead. If you're a nice person, you might consider letting them stay, but somewhere in the process of reading laws and filling out legal forms and driving back and forth to the court house, your bad ass kicks in and you say no. At this point, you can't help them because you've already made a mortgage payment without rent – and you can't make too many of those before they get kicked out, because *you're* losing the house.

Then you get there the day after they move out, and you brace yourself for what's going be inside. You brace yourself for the work it's going to take to get your beautiful investment back in tiptop shape. And once again your bad ass kicks in and you go in and face the music. You just start cleaning – and in my case, learn to take care of the rabbit they left you. In case you're wondering, even at Christmas time, it's hard to give a rabbit away.

After you find a home for the rabbit, and you, your mom, and your friend have spent hours cleaning and taking out trash – and you've secured the contractors in to fix the things that need to be fixed – you realize you are a bad ass. You realize you're willing to do something very few people are. And you realize that you got through it, and that you will make a lot of money. Something else happens – your fear of evicting someone and cleaning up after them goes away.

When that fear dissipates, it doesn't happen again because you simply strap on your bad ass and put your foot down when it starts to go that way. About year and a half after finding the bunny a suitable home, I had another tenant that was falling behind. I had someone who wanted to rent the place, so I asked the current tenant if he wanted out of his lease. He admitted due to personal matters he wasn't able to pay, and we amicably agreed he'd move out at the end of the month. I set up for the new tenants to move in on the first.

The day before the current tenant was supposed to be out, he texted me and said that he would need to stay longer. I told him that was unacceptable, that I had someone coming in the morning to change the locks. He proceeded to threaten me by saying he didn't want to get the cops involved but he was going to. Luckily for me, I earned my bad-ass from the bunny house and I knew, from countless hours preparing eviction documents, what my rights were. I was confident I knew exactly what to do if he wanted me to go the court route.

What is a bad-asses next move? To reply, "I am more than happy to handle this through the court process, however if we do I will go after every cent I am owed, included court costs, back rent, late fees and payment for the broken lease." I didn't get a response, but when I had someone drive by a few hours later, they reported that it looked like a bunch of people were scurrying to move out.

It's often the things you go through that give you the most confidence. I hope you never have to go through an eviction or someone not paying. I hope you take my advice and have a management company handle things for you, but if you do have to go through an eviction, channel your inner bad-ass and know you'll come through better on the other side. I have not had to deal with anyone not paying since.

There's a meme that shows up every once and awhile. It has Neil Patrick Harris on it and it says something to the effect that if you want to have an opinion about my life, then I guess you're going to start paying my bills. As you start to invest in real estate, you'll run into two types of people: those that are envious because they don't have the guts to do what you're doing, and those that have negative feelings about investing in properties. When you run into the person who thinks you're awesome for investing in real estate, stand a little taller and let that soak in. You're doing something most people don't have the guts to do.

When you run into the person who has a negative opinion about you being a real estate investor, or has a snide comment about you being a slumlord, remember why you're doing this. More money, better return on your investment, more control over your money, and because you're a bad ass. Keep your eye on the prize. There were so many times where people had a negative comment or opinion when they'd heard I invested in another place, or that I have investment properties. They didn't bother me for more than two seconds, because I know what my goal is. As I sit here, retired at 32 (and still at 33), I imagine they're all wishing they had the guts to be me.

The more confident I got in real estate investing and my goals, the fewer negative things people said. Somewhere along the way, you realize it's going to work. You're going to achieve your goals, and with that realization, your confidence rises and people start to see you as a smart, savvy, bad-ass investor.

CONCLUSION

If you want to join the bad-ass investor's club, do it. Do your homework, pick a way to get started, and start today. Right now, take a second and ask yourself, "Am I ready to make more money with my money? Am I ready to do something different? Am I ready to take more control of my financial future? Am I ready to become a bad-ass investor?" If you answered yes to any of those questions, congratulations –and welcome to the club. Right now, set the intention for when you want to acquire your first investment. If you know you're going to have to save for a down payment, decide on an amount and set up an automatic transfer to a savings account from your checking account. If you're going to investigate another way of getting started, put it on your calendar to call and ask questions.

One of the things we haven't talked in depth about, yet, is the fact that I retired at 32. For me, my *why*s for investing in real estate are better rates of return and cash flow. I wanted to create a passive cash flow strategy in my life. That was my *why* for investing in real estate. (If you want to know more, you can get my book *Retired at 32* for free here: liveyourchampagnelife.com/investing-gifts)

Beyond a better rate of return and cash flow, my bigger *why* was financial independence. I wanted to have enough passive income to cover my monthly expenses, so I could release my full time job. Part of my bigger *why* is you, right now, reading this book. My biggest *why* for investing in real estate was financial independence, so I could release my job and do what I love. I wanted the time, energy and freedom to create my business, the business that teaches anyone who wants to learn, how to live a Champagne Life.

I didn't have a lot left to give after working 10-12 hours a day, so I sought out a way that I could utilize the money I was making to the best of its ability. I sought out real estate because I saw the potential to create an income that could pay my bills, so I could get on to doing what I'm meant to do.

Now, I'm going to ask you, what is your bigger *why*? Why do you want cash flow or better rates of return? What's the bigger *why*? Being able to retire and enjoy your life? Help send your nieces and nephews to college? Do you have a bigger purpose you want to be fulfilling? Being able to afford to work at a non-profit while still being able to afford to live the life you love? Dream vacations? Taking care of your parents? Having the freedom to do what you desire with your time? Retiring with the ability to travel the world?

What is your bigger *why*? Some people will tell you it has to be a gigantic why, like saving the world. It doesn't. It can simply be the freedom to control your time or your financial future. The more women in this world who have control of their time and have time left over to give, the better. The more women who take control of their financial future, the better. You change the world by identifying your *why* and following through to create your dream.

Knowing your why will keep you on your path. If an investment doesn't work out the way you want, or you have to evict someone, or you have to work harder than you thought for a down payment, or you make a mistake – none of that matters once you get to achieve your big *why*. Trust me, I know.

You have the power to create your deepest desire, quicker than you think. You knew to pick up this book, and you've finished it. You're two steps ahead already. Put your desire out there and watch as what you need next to move forward starts to appear. Listen to your intuition and follow the path that makes sense for you. Get your team on board so you have everything you need to back up your inspiration. Call your accountant. Start asking around for a real estate agent. Get recommendations for a management company. Talk to your real estate agent about classes you can take for investing. Ask them to show you how to calculate the total return on your investment. Bonus: it's better than what I could demonstrate in this book. Start seeking out successful real estate investors to hang out with.

YOU can totally do this. You are smart and successful, and if you want to create financial independence and wealth for yourself, you can. I am so excited for you, and I want to celebrate your success with you. Let me know what's happening. You can email me at spiraluptoday@aol.com.

BONUS CHAPTER
MAKE SURE YOU
READ THIS ONE

If you only read one chapter, make it this one. Here's the deal. I write short books for a reason. My intention is that you can read one of my books in the length of an airplane ride and then you put at least one thing you learned into action.

I also want to make it super easy for you to get the information you need to take that action step, so if you're not an avid reader, and you skipped ahead to this chapter or just skimmed the book, I have an audio for you. I've recorded this book in audio form. It's not word for word me reading it. Rather it's me walking you through the same information I have written in this book. Why? To support you. Not everyone loves to read. Some people learn better from hearing something instead of reading words on the page and some people enjoy the experience of both. I aim to support you anyway I can. You can get the audio by going to liveyourchampagnelife.com/investing-gifts.

I would highly suggest listening to the audio in addition to reading the book.

In this book, I talk about finding your sweet spot. Finding your sweet spot is something I can talk about, but couldn't write about in a way that made sense. I've recorded an audio about how to start finding your sweet spot. You can get that here:

liveyourchampagnelife.com/investing-gifts

In addition to the audios of the book and finding your sweet spot, I am going give you my book *Retired at 32*. *Investing Secrets for a Champagne Life* is the how-to guide, and *Retired at 32* is more of the personal story of how I retired at 32. The one thing *Retired at 32* has in it that *Investing Secrets for a Champagne Life* doesn't, is the Law of Attraction pieces. I am a Deliberate Creator, which means I take responsibility for creating the life I live. I believe our thoughts and our beliefs have a direct impact on our experiences. There is a whole lot of deliberate creation behind my real estate success, and retiring at 32. It's an important piece of the puzzle, but weaving it into this book seemed to muddy the waters. That's why I'm giving you *Retired at 32* and an audio about how I used the Law of Attraction and deliberate creation to get what I wanted, to be financially independent, faster and easier. You can get *Retired at 32* and the Law of Attraction audio here:

liveyourchampagnelife.com/investing-gifts

And I have one more thing for you, an invitation to become part of the Champagne Life Facebook group. This group will support you creating your champagne life. It's a place to celebrate and talk about your champagne life. I'll also be available for some impromptu coaching through the group. It's a great chance to connect those who desire champagne lives and those that are living them! Come on over so we can virtually toast you!

liveyourchampagnelife.com/investing-gifts

Review of Free Gifts:

- Audio version of this book
- Audio about finding your sweet spot
- Copy of my book, *Retired at 32*
- Audio about the role the Law of Attraction played in my financial independence
- Entry into the Champagne Life Facebook group

All available at
liveyourchampagnelife.com/investing-gifts

GLOSSARY OF TERMS

You can research more about any of these terms on the internet. This is just a brief description to add to your understanding while reading the book. Certain terms may have more than one meaning. Those described below are the definitions that correspond to the topic of real estate investing.

Principal Balance - The amount remaining to be paid back on a mortgage loan.

401(k) - Investment vehicle provided by some employers. This has tax advantages you'll want to explore with your CPA or 401(k) administrator.

IRA - Individual Retirement Account.

ROI - Return on investment. It's the amount of money you make on your investment. It's usually calculated by the year. Amount earned/amount invested = ROI.

Financial Independence - Making enough in passive income to cover your monthly expenses.

Passive Income - Income you earn that you don't trade hours for. This can be from investments or from a passive income system you've set up..

Debt to Income Ratio - Percentage of your gross income that goes to paying debts. For example, if you have debt payments of $1000 and you make $2000 a month gross, your debt to income ratio is 50%.

Rate of Return - Similar to ROI. The amount of money you make from your investment. Usually it's calculated annually.

Mortgage - Loan to purchase a house.

Down Payment - The amount of money you pay upfront for a house. It's a percentage required by the loan company.

Appreciation - increase in the value of something, usually a property.

Net Worth - Your assets minus your liabilities.

Assets - Anything that has value.

Liability - Anything you owe, amount of debt.

Net - Money you're making per month after all expenses are paid.

Cash Flow - The amount of money you make from a property after all the expenses are paid.

Fairly Good Credit - Generally anything above 720 credit score is considered good credit.

Deductible - the portion of an insurance claim you have to pay.

Net Operating Expenses - The total of all costs associated with owning and maintaining a property

Owner Occupied - Property where the owner is living in the property.

HELOC - Home Equity Line of Credit

Loan to Value - The amount a property is worth compared to the amount of the loan

RESOURCES

*Resources may vary by area

For Determining Market Rent:
- PadMapper.com
- rentometer.com
- zillow.com

For Finding Properties For Sale:
- zillow.com

For Finding A Realtor:
- LiveYourChampagneLife.com/cool-investment-realtors
- realtor.com

For Creating a Successful Money Mindset:
- Book – Money Mindset for a Champagne Life
- www.moneymoneymoneycourse.com

For Assistance Identifying Your Core Values:
- www.moneymoneymoneycourse.com/manifest/money-money-money-and-core-values-list/

- goodvibeblog.com/know-core-values-for-manifesting-success/
- http://www.annebolender.com/wp-content/uploads/2013/07/eBook-PersonalCore-Values.pdf

For Guidance Identifying Your Investor Label:
- jacqueline-gates.com/radical-re-labeling

ACKNOWLEDGEMENTS

This is more than a book. It's part of my story. And this part of my story wouldn't exist without some amazing people. While there are no words to express the depth of gratitude I feel, I do want to say *thank you* to some important people.

There's not a member of my immediate family who hasn't supported me and my real estate investments. Additionally, Kira and Kayla played a big role. My success is not just about the money. It's about the memories I created along the way. Everything wasn't always easy, but all of you made it more fun. Thank you!

Robyn and JR. You're the best contractor team a girl could ask for. You too, make the story more fun – and I thank you for that.

Thank you Brandon, my amazing realtor, for being not just a great realtor, but a wonderful friend as well.

To my soul friend Lisa, thank you for always celebrating my success with me.

To all of my friends. Part of living a Champagne Life is being surrounded by those you love and adore and who love and adore you. You all are amazing and I thank you for being a part of my life. There are too many of you to list here, but you know who you are.

To my coaching buddies, Jeanette, Jaqui, Janette, Ginny, Laura, Joy, Lainie, Rachel and Melanie. The journey is more fun because we're on it together.

I would also like to thank the entire Your Delicious Book team. You all rock. It's a pleasure to get to work with each and every one of you. Angela, thank you for helping me see how important this book is.

A *very special thank you* to all those who supported my first book launch and helped to make it the success it is. I appreciate all your support.

ABOUT THE AUTHOR

Cassie Parks is a Money Maven. She's dedicated to teaching people how to improve their money mindset to increase their financial success. She's also passionate about real estate investing. Utilizing real estate investing, creating a positive money mindset, and leveraging the power of the Law of Attraction, she retired at 32.

Cassie is the creator of the Money, Money, Money Course. It is the only *pay after you manifest* more money course. She is also the author of *Retired at 32* and *Money Mindset for a Champagne Life*.

Teaching people to live their Champagne Life is one of Cassie's passions. She does this through one-on-one coaching, her Champagne and Coffee group coaching, and speaking or doing interviews about her favorite topics. Speaking to audiences about money mindset, real estate investing, creating your own version of success and self-love are some of her favorite topics.

When Cassie isn't teaching the principles of living a Champagne Life, she can be found enjoying the view from her balcony in Downtown Denver, celebrating with friends over champagne, spending time with her family, traveling, performing Improv, or writing in a local coffee shop.

ABOUT
DIFFERENCE PRESS

Difference Press offers life coaches, other healing professionals, a comprehensive solution to get their book written, published, and promoted. A boutique style alternative to self-publishing, Difference Press boasts a fair and easy to understand profit structure, low priced author copies, and author-friendly contract terms. Founder, Angela Lauria has been bringing the literary ventures of authors-in-transformation to life since 1994.

Your Delicious Book

If you're like many of the authors we work with, you have wanted to write a book for a long time, maybe you have even started a book … or two… or three … but somehow, as hard as you have tried to make your book a priority other things keep getting in the way.

It's not just finding the time and confidence to write that is an obstacle. The logistics of finding an editor, hiring an experienced designer, and figuring out all the technicalities of publishing stops many authors-in-transformation from writing a book that makes a difference. Your Delicious Book is designed to address every obstacle along the way so all you have to do is write!

Tackling the technical end of publishing

The comprehensive coaching, editing, design, publishing and marketing services offered by Difference Press mean that your book will be edited by a pro, designed by an experienced graphic artist, and published digitally and in print by publishing industry experts. We handle all of the technical aspects of your book creation so you can spend more of your time focusing on your business.

Ready to write your book?

Visit www.YourDeliciousBook.com. When you apply mention you are Difference Press reader and get 10% off the program price.

OTHER BOOKS BY DIFFERENCE PRESS

Agile!: The Half-Assed Guide To Creating Anything You Want From Scratch. No Experts Required!
by Sasha Mobley

Fat Be Gone: Four Steps To Permanent Weight Loss And True Happiness by Carleasa Coates
Zen and the Art of Making a Morris Chair: Awaken Your Creative Potential
by Randy Gafner

Craving Love: A Girlfriend's Guide Out of Divorce Hell into Heaven and A New Life You Love
by Shelly Young Modes

Sex, Lies & Creativity: Improve Innovation Skills And Enhance Innovation Culture By Understanding Gender Diversity & Creative Thinking
by Julia Roberts

Woman Overboard! Six Ways Women Avoid Conflict And One Way To Live Drama-Free by Rachel Alexandria

Mafia|Kitten Lessons For Strong Women On Finally Letting Go, Feeling Safe, And Being Loved by Valerie LaPenta Steiger

Tapping Into Past Lives Heal Soul Traumas and Claim Your Spiritual Gifts with Quantum EFT by Jenny Johnston